A RADICAL'S GUIDE TO ECONOMIC REALITY

A RADICAL'S GUIDE TO ECONOMIC REALITY

Angus Black

Holt, Rinehart and Winston, Inc.
New York   Chicago   San Francisco   Atlanta
Dallas   Montreal   Toronto   London   Sydney

Give a capitalist a chance and he'll cop all he can get from society. . . .   But,
at any moment in time, say, tomorrow at 1:43 P.M., the total number of pig grunts, rolls of toilet paper, and acid caps can't get any bigger.

Contents

1 Big Business or Screw the Customer and Full Speed Ahead / 1

2 Our Tax System—A Field Day for the Rich / 5

3 The Draft or You Knew All Along that General Hersheybar Was Full of Shit / 9

4 Hope for Dope / 13

5 The Other America—How Not to Help It / 17

6 Higher Education or Robin Hood Freaks Out / 23

7 Inflation or Whom to Blame for the Rising Cost of Doing Your Thing / 27

8 Why Can't a Woman Be More Like a Man? / 35

9 Unions, Exploitation, or Don't Give Nottin' to Niggers and Wetbacks / 39

10 For Christ's Sake, Stop Eating Grapes! / 43

11 Automation, Technological Unemployment, and the Death of a Workingman / 47

12 The Hidden Persuaders and the Waste Makers or the Decline and Fall of the Affluent Society / 51

13 The War Machine that Keeps Our Country Running / 57

14 Why Can't I Be a Rainmaker Too? / 61

15 Unsafe at Any Speed / 65

16 Danger: This River a Fire Hazard / 69

17 Medical Care: The High Cost of Maintenance and Repairs / 73

18 Rich Nation, Poor Nation / 77

19 The Greatest Show on Earth / 81

20 A Plea for Anarchy / 85

Big Business or Screw the Customer and Full Speed Ahead

Businessmen, especially big businessmen, do whatever they want to you: They set outrageously high prices on their products, bombard you with advertising so that you'll buy something you don't want and didn't even need, and then make sure that what you've bought falls apart just when you get it home. They pay their workers the lowest wages and give them the crappiest working conditions possible.

They use lots of their excess profits to get conservative flunkies elected to the White House and Congress. Then we're told that, yes, it's really true, what's good for General Motors is good for America, even if people are starving and others are working like slaves for 75 cents an hour.

Of this there is no doubt; exploitation and monopoly power exist in this so-called "great land of ours." What may not be so obvious, though, is that our "representative" government has been and continues to be partner to all of this. Only a few courageous presidents have bucked the trend. J.F.K. dared challenge U.S. Steel's unwarranted price increase in 1962. Usually, though, our commanders-in-chief have acted as monopoly mouthpieces. Eisenhower's handling of sagging oil prices serves as a good example. The oil barons didn't like all the cheap stuff that was coming into the U.S. from abroad so able Ike started an oil quota system (which is still probably costing the consumer about $4 billion a year) limiting the amount of oil that could be imported. He told the country that he had to do it for "national security reasons." Any idiot among us could figure out that you can't conserve oil (even for security reasons) by eliminating supplies from outside the country. We ended up doing just the opposite, wiping out reserves at a faster rate than ever before!

Ask any champion of free enterprise like Everett Dirksen or Dwight Eisenhower (Oops! they're dead.) to tell you about the virtues of competition, and you'll soon be overwhelmed by huge quantities of verbal diarrhea. But let some company they're interested in start getting stung by a little foreign competition, and watch out. Barriers will be set up fast and furiously. Soon any remaining resemblance to competition will be purely coincidental.

Big businesses, especially those that have control of an industry, are supposedly prevented from screwing us all. Legally, they can't conspire to set an industry-wide price. A number of laws are on the books—Sherman Anti-Trust, Clayton Act, Robinson-Patman—which the government can use to prosecute such monopoly actions. But time and again government agencies have had the goods on illegal price conspiracies and have done virtually nothing.

One such monopoly case involved two companies that both admitted their illegal actions. Due to buckpassing, personnel changes, and other delays the government didn't hand down a verdict (Guilty, for a change.) until eight years later. By that time the companies had already gone out of business!

A very famous antitrust case of the 1960s involved General Electric and other large electrical manufacturers. It seemed an open-and-shut case. The government had the minutes of all the meetings at which the companies illegally conspired to set industry-wide prices. G.E. had already been involved in over fifteen major U.S. antitrust suits. Was this supergiant smashed? You guessed it. G.E., along with some of the other companies, was merely fined, and a few corporate flunkies got light jail sentences. Our government had every right to break G.E. to bits, as it did Rockefeller's Standard Oil. But there are too many Capitalists walking the halls of the Justice Department for that to happen now.

(Oddly enough, the price-fixing agreements didn't seem to work too well. Prices paid by the guilty companies' customers varied widely soon after every price-fixing meeting. Maybe it was because each Capitalist felt he could make more money screwing the others than by sticking to agreed-on prices. There is no honor among thieves.)

Fearless Dick Nixon, that model of sincerity (Yes, folks, this is the nicest used Chevy that's come through the lot.), is making sure that he'll never be accused of being soft on communism monopolies. He hired Richard W. McLaren, the dumbest lawyer yet to see the back door of the White House, to wage the battle against monopolies. The result: a wave of real and threatened antitrust suits against conglomerates. McLaren's reasons for attacking these diversified giants range from "I don't like bigness" to "The press eats it up." Will the public benefit from the campaign against bigness? Maybe. But we'd certainly get more from the Justice Department if it used its powers to eliminate true monopolies and organized crime. We can easily view the history of this great body of learned lawyers as the path of least resistance with the most publicity.

We can also view the history of judicial and Congressional actions aimed at protecting the consumer from Capitalist greed as a history of government-sponsored monopolies. Federal, state, and local governments have created far more monopolies than they've destroyed.

Why is the piece of paper telling some Capitalist that he can send out radio or T.V. signals worth so many hundreds of thousands of dollars? Because the Federal Communications Commission makes sure that competition does not exist in the production of these signals.

Why does a flight from Los Angeles to San Francisco cost less than one of about equal distance between, say, Boston and New York City? Because the Civil Aeronautics Board keeps up monopoly power in air transportation *between* states but not *within* states.

Why can the owner of a piece of metal saying he can operate a cab in New York City easily sell the medallion for $26,000? Because the government of the City of New York creates a monopoly position for these medallion owners by issuing very few of the medallions and refusing to add more. Otherwise there'd be many times the number of taxis in the city than there are today.

Ask the government to help the consumer and you're asking for a bigger and bigger system of special-interest groups screwing the public. This is one request that's seldom denied.

Our government's inability to prevent Capitalists from doing what they damn well please extends to its impotence at getting any of their ill-earned billions.

Our Tax System — A Field Day for the Rich

You're probably saying to yourself by now, why don't we tax the shit out of all those Capitalist bastards? Mr. Government Stooge will immediately show you our progressive income tax rates and say, "But we are. After all, anybody who makes over $100,000 can only keep 30 cents of every dollar he makes over that amount, and besides there were relatively ten times more millionaires being taxed in 1929 than today. So there are fewer rich people today."

The chance of the last statement being true is about as great as the chance of a catnip high turning into a two-day trip.

The reason so few people report *taxable* income of a

million dollars or more today is because they've hired sharp tax lawyers who make sure every conceivable legal loophole and dodge is used. The dozen or so Capitalists who make the news each year because they pay no taxes at all on their millions give us a clue as to how widespread this legalized swindling actually is.

Let's see how progressive our taxes really are. In 1966 total individual income was $468 billion after deductions; taxable income from returns was $285 billion. The government copped $56 billion of it. A little simple arithmetic shows that it wound up with less than 20 percent of taxable income.

Since it has been so profitable for Capitalists to find more and more weak points in the tax laws, they've done so. We now have oil depletion allowances, low capital gains rates, and big business deductions added to the Internal Revenue's books. To think Capitalists would act otherwise is to deny the undeniable fact that they'll cop all they can get. To think that Congress will effectively change the situation is to deny reality. How many poor Senators do you know?

Let's quit fooling ourselves. Get rid of the progressive income tax. In its place put a flat 20 percent tax on all income over a certain minimum, while eliminating all escape clauses. We'll end up getting more from the rich than now, for it will no longer be worth it to them to cheat and look for legal loopholes with the aid of lawyers. As an added attraction those high-paid tax lawyers will then be out of their jobs. Their salaries may suffer, and so more legal aid might be funneled to defending the poor in our rich man's system of "justice."

Getting rid of our present income tax mess would also save taxpayers a wad. How? By eliminating the time and effort that they and their accountants spend on filing returns. In a recent study the American Bar Association came up with the estimate that we had put a preposterous $1.3 billion of effort into filing 1967 returns.

It's not hard to guess why. Ever try to read the 1954 Internal Revenue Code? Ever try merely to figure out the do-it-yourself books on filling out tax returns? One young professor of taxation and public finance spent days filling out his form 1040. He proudly sent it in expecting a fat refund in exchange for all his efforts at cracking the tax game. Several weeks later the I.R.S. computer sent him a short note explaining that he hadn't done anything right—his refund was cut in half. How the hell can the guy on the street ever hope to do things right?

Of course this tax reform I've proposed will not help the poor, black or white. Something else must be added to it, but more on that later. I don't like to cross my bridges before they hatch.

The Draft or You Knew All Along that General Hersheybar Was Full of Shit

Many an American Capitalist, especially a Northern one, can sit back and reflect on the great freedoms bestowed on us all. True, we did have slavery before, but that's been outlawed.

False! We still have slavery in the U.S., only it's now called the draft. General Hersheybar had his own unique way of putting it before Nixon canned him. He said that a voluntary draft was impossible, so we have to rely on patriotism; therefore we draft!

Who pays the price of this slavery? As always, the slaves. True, according to some, they get certain benefits. (My father is still waiting for me to be drafted so I'll become a man.) The fact is that draftees are paying an enormous price whether they're drafted by lottery or by the old way. It's roughly equal to the difference between what men could earn as civilians and what they get from the Army. I say roughly because I'm sure the Army would have to pay them much more to eat crap and take shit from would-be Napoleons voluntarily.

Draftees are not the only ones who pay. We all do. We're denied the knowledge of the *true* cost of our Vietnams and Dominican Republics. The true cost of a soldier to society is what he could contribute as a civilian. This can be roughly measured by what he would be paid. So the cost of the 3 million plus soldiers to society is what they could have earned in civilian life. You don't read about it, but we're paying a lot more for Vietnam than most people imagine.

Hersheybar seemed to have it all wrong. A volunteer Army in place of our current slave system would solve many problems. If the pay were high enough to get all the necessary soldiers, the real cost of Vietnam would be known to all. There might then be fewer Capitalists willing to support our imperialism.

The draft also makes the Army more costly than it would be if it were all volunteers. The turnover rate among 18-26-year-olds in the service is higher with the present system than it would be with a volunteer one, so that more is being spent than need be in getting our men up to the desired killing capacity.

Many have disagreed with the idea of a purely volunteer Army, claiming that we won't be able to get enough soldiers when we need them "at any price." If high pay can't attract sufficient volunteers to fight in Vietnam that means something —Americans are not willing to continue genocide in Southeast Asia.

Also there's a cost borne by all males who alter their life plans in order to avoid the draft. How many of you reading this would have gone directly from high school to college if you had had a free choice? Whatever happened to that year of bumming around Europe or just plain dropping out? How about all those physicists who really wanted to study modern literature or those engineers who dreamed of being ski instructors? How many of your old high-school buddies, the guys who always stood in line first for a gang bang, have suddenly looked to God for help and are now theological students? And by the way, do you know anyone whose current address is Canada? Or whose name is no longer his own?

The government doesn't force people to become tax collectors, Federal marshalls (Red, white, and blue pigs?), or garbage collectors. Why then does it have to draft cannon fodder?

Hope for Dope

Government officials, pig officials, school officials, and parents are fond of bringing the drug problem into their cocktail party conversations. Typically, as the party becomes more lively, the drunker ones start really getting down to the nitty-gritty: "Those goddam kids aren't worth shit these days. The police have got to put a stop to pot-smoking, put all them dope users in jail. How can America remain great if we let our kids turn into useless drug addicts?" The last remark is usually uttered by someone just as he's about to vomit, pass out, or both.

Drugs, you've been told a million times, is one of the biggest problems facing America today. But wait a minute. There are more alcoholics than drug addicts. Why aren't we more worried about the booze problem?

You know the answer as well as I do. An alcohol high is usually legal; a pot high, sunshine high, or speed high isn't. But how can that be? The destruction of the body due to too much alcohol is certainly better documented than the injurious effects of pot. The drunken driver is certainly as much of a hazard to society as the stoned hippie sitting in his bedroom staring at the ceiling.

Why the hell isn't a liquid high judged as bad for America as any other high?

We all know that at one time it was. Prohibition was one of the government's most far-reaching attempts at legislation to control society's moral behavior. What happened during those great days of the speakeasy and Al Capone? People that wanted a drink got one, but at an absurdly high cost. Besides risking jail, paying high prices, and knowing they were doing something illegal, many whisky heads also got sick, were blinded, or died. Why? Because of the horrible crap that certain Capitalists put in their bottles.

Did Prohibition last? How could it, for even some of the most righteous Congressmen liked to drink once in a while (and still do). In spite of the very strict Volstead Act, law enforcement proved impossible. The period 1919 to 1933 was one of rampant bootlegging and unparalleled drinking. People came to the inevitable conclusion that drinking wasn't so bad for society after all. The liquid high became legal again with the ratification of the 21st amendment.

Just as liquor prohibition was wrong and couldn't last, so grass prohibition is wrong and cannot last. Some Congressmen may want to turn on too someday (if that sweet smell can't already be detected occasionally in those fancy Washington, D.C., suburbs). The similarity between our current drug "problem" and the liquor problem of the twenties is striking. Ours is a period of rampant pushing and unparalleled dropping, shooting up, and smoking.

Just as a criminal underground thrived on illegal distribution of booze in the twenties, so one thrives today on illegal distribution of pot, acid, speed, horse, snow, and sunshine.

Just as drinkers in the twenties sometimes bought high-priced poison in whisky bottles, so trippers today sometimes buy high-priced poison in sugar cubes, whites, reds, and blues.

I'm sure you're wondering why we don't still read about drinkers occasionally getting a little wood alcohol in their bottles and consequently going blind. The reason, oddly enough, is due to greedy Capitalists all trying to make the most money from the public.

During Prohibition the number of dealers in booze was much more limited than after 1933. Why? Because the game was too risky with the Feds ready to jump on you at any minute. The police payoff costs were staggering, and the jail sentences could be long if you got caught.

Could the owner of the illegal speakeasy ever advertise publicly the quality of his liquor to attract more customers? Could a whisky producer put up billboards proclaiming that he had foolproof quality control? Was anybody sure that the label on his bottle meant anything at all?

Today things are different—so different, in fact, that the booze hound never has to worry about being poisoned by his can of Bud or his shot of Seagram's 7. Why? Because of greedy Capitalist producers. They know that their brand-named liquor won't sell if people find out about an occasional pinch of rat poison slipping into the brewing vats. And if people don't find out about it on their own, competitors will soon let the public know.

What can you do today when your last trip proved a bummer because that shit you dropped was cut with finely ground Draino? Very little. You can buy it from another pusher the next time, but you'll still be taking your chances. Since the whole scene's illegal, there's not much advertising on billboards and in shops for brands of acid or grass that assure you of high quality. The government has fixed things so that you have a greater chance of freaking out during any trip. How? By making certain not enough money-hungry Capitalists are competing for your drug dollars.

Private interests are also helping to keep up the status

quo. You wouldn't believe the bread liquor-makers are spending on lobbies against legalized grass. The tobacco companies are a little smarter. They know the inevitable will come. It's rumored that they've got lease options on thousands of acres of prime grass lands in Mexico. They know that when pot's legal a hell of a lot more people are going to smoke it. They're making sure their share of the supply will be big enough.

What should the role of our government be in the whole drug question (Drug meaning caffeine, alcohol, tobacco, pot, aspirins.)? I say only as a provider of information. If people want to know how harmful cigarette smoking is, they can read government statistics on the cancer rate among tobacco freaks. If people don't want their kids to smoke they can educate them as to its bad effects. The same goes for drinking. It's a tribute to the large payoffs from the liquor industry that we rarely read about the harm that comes from boozing it up.

If parents don't want their kids to turn on, let them be the educators. At the most, let the government be the provider of relevant, truthful, scientific information in this area, as well as others.

No government has the right to tell me how to run my private life so long as I do not physically injure others. The laws against pot, sixty-nining, homosexuality, prostitution, and gambling must be struck from the books.

To each man his own bag.

The Other America — How Not to Help It

Them that's got shall get;
Them that's not shall lose,
So the Bible says,
And it still makes news . . .

Poverty existed yesterday; poverty exists today; and poverty will exist tomorrow if "something" isn't done about it. What have Americans done so far to help the poor?

Well, we saw that farmers seemed to be poor during the Depression, so we helped them by fixing high prices for their products. This caused them to produce more (it's almost as if they were acting like Capitalists and grabbing all they could get). But consumers wouldn't buy all that the farmers were growing at their new high prices. The solution was simple: The government had to buy the excess and store it. To keep the storage bill down the government decided to pay farmers *not* to grow on some of their land and to plow under some of their crops. But farmers aren't stupid. At the new high prices it paid them to use more fertilizer on the remaining legally usable land. They ended up producing more.

I could go on forever about what has happened with a program that was originally set up to give the poor farmer a higher income. Now we see that the amount of help they get is directly in proportion to how *large,* not how small, their resources and incomes are. The rich get rich and the poor supposedly get welfare.

State welfare payments (which are Federally subsidized) are intended to help the poor. They are given out by highly-paid busybodies who make sure that recipients are spending the money in a manner that will please middle-class holier-than-thous. The system makes sure that men who want to work don't, by requiring the absence of a working male in all ADC households. To insure that ADC mothers are not getting any on the side, night-prowling snoops are hired to spy on them.

It was felt that housing should be made cheaper for the poor. So we got cheap public hi-rises, now referred to as Congo Hiltons by their inhabitants. Since slums are the most obvious aspect of poor housing, the government gave us urban renewal. It was soon obvious that the spelling was wrong. It's Negro removal. The greatest effect of this governmental black banishment has been to raise honky house values.

New York's Mayor Lindsay showed that he was concerned about high housing costs. He threatened more rent controls if landlords didn't stop raising their rents. What he failed to realize was a fundamental economic reality: New York's current housing crisis is due precisely to rent controls! Capitalists are always faced with deciding where they can screw the public the most. Never give a sucker an even break seems to be their motto. When they realized that with rent controls they couldn't make as much profit by building apartments in New York as, say, by building them in L.A., they naturally stopped building in N.Y. The result—a critical housing shortage where people are continually outbidding each other to get a place to live. And the people don't always outbid one another by merely offering to pay apartment owners something under the table; extra payment is often extended on the bed.

Recently, a government official gave his solution to the whole poverty problem: Raise the minimum wage to $2 an hour and make it stick for all workers. The Reverend Martin Luther King, Jr., also offered this as a solution to the black man's economic misery.

Minimum wages seem the perfect way of stopping Capitalists from exploiting the poor. If we look carefully at situations where minimum wages exist, we will see that this may not always be the case. Sometimes even the opposite is true, and this would-be cure only serves to make the problem worse.

You must realize that while a minimum wage tells a Capitalist what he has to pay a worker, there is no law that says he has to hire any *specific number* of workers. If the skills and talents you can offer someone are worth $1 an hour to him, but he's required to pay you $1.50, will he hire you? Hell no, because then he'd be screwing himself. He'd rather hire fewer workers or buy a machine.

Besides, it becomes more and more profitable to automate, as the minimum wage gets relatively higher and higher. (This also might hold true of some union wage tactics.) Be careful of falling into the trap of thinking that Capitalists won't be able to substitute machines for men. The long-run tendency for this to happen is pretty obvious. It can also happen fairly rapidly, as in the case of the elevator operators. They all got together and decided they weren't being paid enough, so they refused to work unless they got a much higher salary. In a few short years there were automatic elevators in all cities where operators had refused to work for the previous low wages.

The dramatic 15 percent unemployment rate among black teenagers today can be tied directly to the increasing minimum wage set by Congress. I agree that anything less than the minimum wage is inhuman, but shouldn't someone who can't sell his labor for high pay, often due to forces beyond his control, at least be given the opportunity to work for lower pay if he chooses? Why should I tell him that I'd rather see him unemployed?

All these examples merely serve to show that we're not getting rid of poverty in any significant manner with our present programs.

The realistic solution is simple. People are poor because they don't have much money. They don't have much because Capitalists don't value their labor very highly. So, as a first step, give them money. But don't attach middle-class strings to it, because when you do, somebody will screw up the works. Why should we try to decide who the "worthy" poor are. The black poor, the farm poor, the stoned poor, the straight poor—they're all equally worthy of getting money by means of a negative income tax or some sort of minimum income.

Why should the government be plowing several million dollars into an experiment in New Jersey in order to see if the poor who get "free" money will spend it in the "right" way? Why should cities be given grants just for the purpose of determining who the worthy poor are and how they'll spend the money that may be given to them?

Granted, it would be nice if politicians could show the middle class that the lower class will try their damnedest to take on the "right" values. But let's face it, Capitalists like to talk dollars and cents. They know that the current ridiculous aid schemes are costing them a wad. By simply giving low or no income families money, we could cut out much waste of tax dollars and we would all be better off.

A highly respected member of the Budget Bureau got the figures together on how much was being spent on all poverty programs. He then calculated the total cost of direct payments to all families necessary to bring everyone above the "poverty line." The conclusion he reached was that direct income payments would add up to less than half the present poverty-help outlays! Even the Wallace supporter around the corner may be convinced by the tax savings to him that unworthy niggers, hippies, artists, and bums should all get a minimum income, too.

Another important benefit of direct minimum income payments would be a renewed sense of dignity for the current welfare poor. We also could eliminate the numerous political connections so often tied to welfare and other such programs (as occur daily in Daleyland, U.S.A.). Think, too, of all those snooping social workers who will be forced to do something worthwhile, like teaching.

Notice that giving people money will not help them get into the American mainstream (hopefully, nothing will). Without looking into the sociology of poverty, one thing remains clear. If we could somehow help poor people earn more money, they would no longer be poor. How do we do this? Ask businessmen to be good heads? Crap. Did you ever see a Capitalist do something nice if there wasn't a buck in it for him?

Maybe we should have the government be the "employer of last resort"? Again, crap. Then we would eventually see Fascist officials checking up on how the wages were being spent.

The way to a businessman's heart is through his wallet. Make poor people more valuable to him. How? Educate them.

Higher Education or Robin Hood Freaks Out

It's a well-founded cliché that you can't get more out of something than you put into it. When more is put into a poor man, we can then expect a businessman to be willing to pay more for his work. Why don't we put more into the black poor, white poor, yellow poor, speed poor. How? By offering more and better educational opportunities for these so-called culturally disadvantaged (Whitey's name for everyone he's exploited).

It's obvious from looking at precollege financial statistics that more is spent on each pupil outside ghettos than in them. The solution? Have the government build better schools in the ghetto? This would be the kiss of death, for who would remain in control of these new schools? Middle-class Fascists trying to impose their values on everybody around. The only meaningful solution has been given by a group of unreal but daring conservatives. They suggest we give every parent every year for every school-age kid a certificate with the following words:

> Here is $1000 that can be spent only on education in any school of your choice. Pick your school wisely, for the kid you save is your own.

Of course, we would have to allow more private schools to exist. Today, if you don't like the way your kids are being educated, you can take them to a private school; but you still pay taxes for the public ones. Most people can't afford to foot this bill twice, so we have few private schools. When everyone is given a free choice on where to spend his educational tax dollars (certificates), watch out. The stampede away from the present public schools will run you over.

Your first reaction may be, shit it won't work. But it did, right after the Korean War. We called it the G.I. Bill and used it only for college education. No one can deny the huge success of that "certificate" program.

If it's obvious that the poor are getting screwed with primary and secondary education, it should also be obvious that the story's the same with so-called higher education. Before you stand up to sing your Alma Mater, let's look at a few facts.

Every state has "free" colleges for its residents. These great institutions are supported largely by state taxes and Federal money (which pays, by the way, for a large part of our offensive research). Anybody who qualifies can attend. But what are the qualifications? Good grades. And who usually makes good grades? Rich kids and brown nosers (usually the same people). The direct relation between levels of school achievement and socioeconomic background is one of the best documented facts in educational research.

Think also about the true cost of college to the student. The greatest cost to him is not the money he puts in for books and fees but the money he could have made had he not chosen to have all the education he could get. These sacrificed earnings loom a little larger in the mind of a seventeen-year-old with four younger brothers and a drunk, out-of-work father than they do in the mind of a seventeen-year-old whose dad makes forty-eight grand a year selling napalm for Dow Chemical.

A few casual observations will show how right I am. Kids from poor families don't usually blow four years basking in the sun at U.C.L.A. Along this line, a magazine article of a few years back gave the incredible information that the average family income of Berkeley students was well over $10,000 in the early 1960s. Many laughed at this "obvious exaggeration." For these doubting Thomases I would like to tell a little story.

When the War on Poverty program was first formed, its members had the brilliant idea of helping out poverty-stricken students at state universities. The University of California at Berkeley was awarded $254,000 for this purpose. A work-study program was set up. Recruiting notices first appeared, informing all those needy students from families earning less than $3000 a year of their new money-making opportunity. Apparently the initial response was rather meager, to say the least. The requirements became looser and looser. Eventually a friend of mine even made the grade. He was French, without American citizenship, and his parents had never known an income as low as $3000.

And so goes the governmental Robin Hood, robbing tax dollars from the poor for the education of the rich.

The public is really getting shafted with undergraduate education, but this is nothing compared to what is happening at the graduate level. Many people put forward the argument that we should subsidize college education because of its side effects (if you have the misfortune of talking to an economist, he'll call them externalities). We're all better off because educated kids vote more intelligently (as if that ever made any difference) or don't kill as much. This might be an argument for subsidizing general undergraduate education. But can it apply to subsidizing highly specialized advanced degrees?

P.H.D.'s typically spend three–ten years acquiring knowledge in narrow fields. They are amply rewarded with fat paychecks for their hard work of passing exams and writing theses on topics so trivial that a listing of them would make a hit broadway comedy. Why can't these cats pay their own way?

If that isn't enough, those who remain in academia are subsidized while continuing their work on such interesting subjects as mating characteristics of the West Bornian tree hog and the effects of zero temperature on astrological predictions. To make sure politics can't interfere with this courageous work, they set up a guaranteed retirement system and call it tenure.

What should be done? A form of G.I. bill for everyone could be offered. At the same time, we should stop all direct public monopoly operation in higher education. The "certificates" may not be large enough to cover living expenses. But that's no problem. The government could provide loans at the going rate. The reason students will be able to repay these loans in later years is that they will earn higher salaries because of their education. For once the government would give everyone a fair and equal chance.

Let's get Robin Hood to a rescue center quick so he can pull out of his bad trip.

Inflation or Whom to Blame for the Rising Cost of Doing Your Thing

As the number of joints you can buy with your panhandled dollar gets smaller and smaller, you probably begin to suspect that the rising cost of living has finally gotten to you. Why does the price of everything have to keep going up? Why can't the government do something to the bastards who keep charging higher and higher prices? What's causing this mess? Many explanations have been given and more are yet to come. None will change the sad state of things though.

You might know some fat cat who can't understand why he's fat, and why he keeps getting fatter. He's probably gone to his family doctor who told him it was because of nerves and prescribed some pills. If the fat cat still keeps on getting fatter he'll probably go to a specialist who will run all kinds of expensive tests and come to the conclusion that the problem is either glands or metabolism. Other specialists could probably come up with even more sophisticated reasons. I'm sure you would know all along that no matter what else, the fat cat won't stop getting fatter until he starts eating less. Why did he get fat in the first place? Simply because he took in more calories than his body used up. You are what you overeat.

So what does this have to do with inflation?

Everything. Our inflation is simply a fat price level getting fatter.

Why?

Because the economy is being fed too much.

Fed what?

Fed dollars.

By whom?

By the Federal Reserve System (commonly known as the Fed by knowledgeable economists).

People can't spend more than they have—at least not for very long. Any dollar you spend somebody else gets, and any dollar you get someone else spends. For all of us put together this simply means that the total amount spent is equal to the total amount received. (Unless, of course, someone is doing his thing with a basement printing press.)

What is spent merely equals the number of dollars floating around multiplied by the number of times they change hands. What is received simply equals the number of things sold multiplied by their prices.

Since these two equals equal, the relationship between prices and other things can easily be figured out. Say dollar bills don't change hands faster than usual and that there aren't more things being bought than usual. Then, if the number of dollars floating around increases, prices have nowhere to go but up. How do these excess dollars come into existence? Because someone is doing his thing with a printing press, but not in a damp dark basement. It's happening in the well-lit offices of the U.S. Treasury and Federal Reserve, Washington, D.C., 20551.

Every time anyone has looked at different periods of inflation, in this country or others, the statistics have always shown a relatively large increase in the number of dollars (pesos, rubles, etc.) around. It's true that sometimes this increase is made worse by businessmen and other people changing their financial habits, but for the most part government behavior has been the culprit.

What does this mean?

The government causes inflation by making available too many pieces of paper with pictures of slave-owning national heroes printed on them. And, of course, some of us don't like to see money sitting around idle so we spend it.

It's an undeniable fact that when more people want something than is available, like tickets to *Hair*, they bid up the price. It's also undeniable that when more is around of something than people want, like plastic Christs that glow in the dark, they don't value it so highly. What is the value of a dollar to you? It's probably at least equal to what you can trade it for, so the dollar prices of things should reflect the value of your dollars. If the supply of those dollars goes up drastically they'll probably be worth less; that is, you won't be able to trade them for as much stuff anymore, and so—the rising cost of living.

I'm sure you're saying that this idea of inflation is too simple. After all, that great intellectual L.B.J. got the best economists in the country to be on his Council of Economic Advisers. Why didn't they see the plain and unadorned truth? My own theory is that before they joined the team they were required to go through a solemn initiation ceremony during which they all swallowed pills that destroyed their minds for the duration of their appointments. Also, put yourself in the position of the highly paid specialist. Will your patients pay you to tell them simply to eat less?

When asked what he thought caused inflation, the Mormon's answer to Bobby Kennedy, George Romney, said he thought it was high interest rates. L.B.J.'s economic wisdom yielded the same brilliant conclusion. He cried out in anger at the Federal Reserve System for raising their interest rates "on the eve of Christmas spending." How unchristian.

In the first place, both men failed to realize that inflation *causes* high interest rates, and not the other way around. Let's imagine that an evil fairy turned you into a banker. Prices have been going up 5 percent a year for ten years. An acid head comes in off the street and wants to borrow $100 for a year. You figure out your costs for giving the loan. You decide that you'd make out okay if you charged 3 percent or $3 for the loan. Is that what you'd really charge? You'd be crazy, if you expected the inflation to continue at 5 percent a year. Because if it does, $100 one year from now will only be worth $95 in purchasing power. If you only charged $3 for the loan, and even if the acid head did repay you at the end of the year, you'd wind up with less than you started with.

In addition to all your regular loan-making expenses, you'd also have to cover the decreased value of those dollars loaned out. So you'd probably charge about $8 or 8 percent. Why 8 percent and not 3 percent? Because experience has taught you that the cost of living will probably keep rising at the rate of 5 percent a year. Who's causing this rise? As always, the government, by feeding too much money into the economy.

I'm sure you've probably heard that "a little inflation is a good thing." Don't believe a word of it. To say that a little steady inflation is a good thing because it promotes higher employment, buoyant spirits, and so on is to say that all businessmen are stupid and that all workers are terribly slow in realizing what's happening. A great man, I think it was Bob Dylan, once said you can't fool all the people all the time. If the government printing presses cause prices to rise at 5 percent per year, year in and year out, won't businessmen begin to expect the trend to continue? Won't unions begin to expect it also, and demand wages that rise to cover the rising cost of living? Won't at least some nonunion workers demand that they, too, get wage increases to cover the inflationary erosion of their paychecks?

The evidence answers yes to all those questions. In countries with steady, predicted inflation, all prices, including those we call wages, adjust step-by-step with the rising cost of living. This just tells you that you can't fool workers into working for falling *real* wages (money wages divided by the rising cost of living or what you can really buy with your money) even though this could get rid of unemployment. With prices rising faster than wages, Capitalists end up exploiting workers more. Capitalists would therefore be willing to hire more workers— so less unemployment.

The only way for this to work is to fool everyone continuously by continually changing the rate of inflation in some unpredictable fashion. The U.S. government has done just this at times. Since the cost of living rises sometimes at a fast rate, sometimes at a slow rate nobody can adjust things completely. Since people were fooled, the economy suffered from sometimes overheating, sometimes underheating.

Many people like to blame the big businessmen for inflation. It's easy to see that they're the ones who raise prices. They in turn blame increasing labor costs, brought about by excessive union demands.

We all know that Capitalists charge the highest prices possible. But we also know that not all of them are stupid. Some will set prices which enable them to make higher profits than others who set different prices. These higher profits cannot be hidden for long. The rest then will soon follow suit, and charge a similar price so that they, too, can get in on the killing. Since not all customers are stupid, some will buy from the guys selling at the lowest prices. Those selling at a higher price will start losing a few well-informed customers. If they don't fall into line with their competitors, they may eventually start losing money and might even go out of business, any Capitalist's nightmare.

Although Capitalists would like to set high prices, some

of them find they actually make more money by asking less, because they get more customers that way. As every business-man, by definition, tries to make as much money as he can, prices charged for any given product tend to be about the same.

You might agree with this for a so-called competitive industry, but you're probably thinking that I can't be talking about steel producers or car manufacturers. After all, we know that those monopolists don't have any competition, do they? That may be true, but they still can't set any price they wish. Why? Because some people will refuse to buy their products.

Look at steel. Let U.S. Steel double its prices and Boeing will start using more aluminum and plastic in their 747's. Let G.M., Ford, Chrysler, and American Motors double the price of their cars, and more people will start buying foreign cars, riding motorcycles and bikes, taking buses, or walking. Even a pure monopolist has limits—the number of available substi-tutes—set on the prices of his product.

There's probably nothing in the world that doesn't have some substitute.

Look at electricity, something we can't do without. In most parts of the country this monopoly is regulated by a commis-sion of men who make sure the public isn't getting it in the ear. On second thought, though, doesn't electricity have sub-stitutes? For heating purposes people can and do use wood, coal, oil, and natural gas instead of electricity. Do huge manu-facturing plants have to buy electricity? No, they can generate their own, and many do when the outside price of electricity becomes too steep. So even this monopoly has price limits set by available substitutes.

What usually happens is that the regulated electricity companies and their regulators realize they are dependent on one another for their existence. So they conspire to dupe the public. In many states, for example, as soon as the utility com-panies make a cost-lowering discovery, they tell the commis-sion that they want to decrease prices (in order to compete better with the substitutes). The commissioners make a statement to the press that the public deserves a price cut. The companies scream bloody murder, but reluctantly carry out the commission's orders.

Even if this crap didn't go on, in an inflationary setting the public will suffer from the price regulation of monopolies. The regulators don't change prices fast enough to keep up with the ever-changing situation. At the resulting artificially low prices the only way for the monopolists to keep their profits up (which you can be sure they will do) is by limiting production. The monopolist will then produce less than the public wants. (He can also lower quality.) The result will be a shortage. We only need look at telephone service in some under-developed countries (and also N.Y.C.). Since the telephone companies there cannot legally raise their prices, they haven't increased telephone service in years. Try to get a phone in Lima or Mexico City. You have to wait until somebody who already has one dies.

J.F.K.'s anger at U.S. Steel's increase in prices should have been directed at the Federal Reserve System. If our latest inflation hadn't been continually stuffed by the Fed, it would have stopped. But because it was stuffed, U.S. Steel, just like all other companies, was setting its prices at a level that yielded the greatest profits. In an inflationary situation that level happens to be constantly rising.

When you read statements like the one in *Time* about the inflation in Brazil being so great that money printing presses couldn't keep up with it, laugh. The reason inflation continues is simply *because of* the printing press's hyperactivity.

So watch out for that perfect set-up of a job with a guar-anteed fixed income for the next ten years. At the rate the price level's gaining weight, your future years will be mighty lean.

Why Can't a Woman Be More Like a Man?

If a woman hasn't been convinced by her father, brothers, lovers, and husband that she is inferior, she'll certainly have no doubts remaining after looking for work. The discrimination against females in the job market is widespread and well-known. The government wants to put a stop to it all; equal pay for equal work. In its never-ending fight against discrimination the government has declared illegal any advertising for jobs on the basis of sex.

Women can now breathe a long sigh of relief. Their days of unfair treatment at the hands of unfair Capitalists are numbered. But are they? Let's look behind Capitalists' attempts at putting the working girl down.

When an employer has to replace someone or must fill a new job he realizes that a certain amount of training will have to be invested in whomever he hires. Obviously, though, less time is required to teach a ditchdigger what to do than to show a telephone repairman how to fix a Princess.

In any event, every Capitalist realizes that something will have to be spent on training his new employees. As always, he wants to get the most for his money. How does he do it? By hiring someone he thinks will give him the greatest return on his investment.

Let's take an example. Suppose Mr. Rich builds power boats. He's been doing so well he wants to build even more than before, so he decides to add a nighttime work shift at his plant. Naturally he needs more workers. He puts an ad in the paper. There is a large response—applications from 23 men and 6 women. But he only needs 18 new workers. How does he decide whom to hire? He'll want the people from whom he thinks he'll get the best work. But he also knows that he doesn't want workers who may quit on him in 2 months' time. After all, he figures he'll be paying them much more than they're worth for at least 3 weeks, that is, until the time they have learned their new jobs well.

That means three weeks of investing in 18 new workers. If any of them quit right away his investment will walk out the door. Experience has taught him that women tend to stay on the job less long than men. We all know why. Single girls get married and quit. Married women get pregnant and quit. And they both change their minds all the time.

At the same wages will Mr. Rich hire any of the women, even if they're as well-qualified as the men? Probably not, for he's surer of recouping his investment in men. How can women ever expect to get a job? Easily, by working for less; lower pay for equal work. Unfair? Maybe, but only to those females who really are stable workers. They'll soon get equal pay for equal work anyway.

Given the chance, a Capitalist will hire a person who will give the most work for the longest time. Since women usually have very good reasons for not working as long as men, they wind up either accepting lower pay or putting out for the boss in order to get jobs. Government orders to the contrary will not change the sad facts.

Women's usually short stay in the job market presents society with a problem concerning their education. Most people think we should have an educated public, thus we subsidize education. The spillover (side effects) argument that I mentioned before can really only be used for a liberal arts education. People are amply rewarded for any efforts at specialized training. Society subsidizes both general and specialized education, though. It costs the same to get your B.A. in the humanities as it does in engineering.

When a smart chick decides to become an engineer and to take advantage of "free" state education, she ends up taking away an engineering degree from someone else, probably a guy. (The number of spaces in any engineering school is limited in any one year.) Let's assume she does well and gets a good job after graduation. So far, so good.

After three years of musical beds, our woman engineer may decide to marry, settle down, and have kids. She stops working. Society takes it in the ear. Why? Because public money was invested in subsidizing the training of a highly specialized female instead of a guy. The female used her training fewer years than a male counterpart probably would have. The return on society's investment was much less than it could have been.

For this reason I suggest, in the context of our present situation, that we require females who get specialized degrees at "free" colleges either to work as long as their male counterparts, or pay back in full to the state the cost of their specialized training.

If a woman were more like a man, she'd be treated as such.

Unions, Exploitation, or Don't Give Nottin' to Niggers and Wetbacks

Anybody who's read Marx knows that workers are exploited. What they produce is worth more than they're paid. Workers have always known that the Boss has been taking advantage of them; that's why they form unions. By banding together and agreeing not to work for low pay any longer union members have attempted to cash in on some of those misplaced profits. The important question is: Have they been successful? If you ask them, they will surely say yes. After all, wages are higher now than ever before. We realize that part of this increase has been due to inflation, and therefore doesn't make any difference. (If all prices go up 20 percent and so does my pay, am

I better off?) But the rest is real; that is, the workers' standard of living is in fact higher today than ever before.

You should be suspicious, though, about the possibility of a Capitalist allowing any of his profits to slip through his fingers in the meantime. Do you remember what happened when the elevator operators got together and refused to work for low pay? Every downtown building that could do so installed an automatic elevator. This should give some idea of how Capitalists can avoid helping workers out. In situations where complete automation is impossible they merely hire fewer workers. The great John L. Lewis understood this economic reality perfectly: "It is better to have half a million men working at good wages and high standards of living than to have a million working in poverty and degradation."

Lewis understood a fundamental aspect of Capitalists' behavior: They consider labor as if it were steel, coal, or lumber. Therefore, when the price is raised, they buy less. It's probably true that we don't see this happen immediately after any price rise of labor or products. But the sad truth will hit some of the workers, sooner or later.

What union men try to do, then, is raise their wages relative to those of nonunion workers. Historical evidence shows that they haven't always been too successful. Since union members sometimes succeed in getting wages that are higher than they would be without bargaining, employers wind up wanting fewer workers.

It is the union that must somehow ration the scarce number of jobs to a group of more-than-willing workers. One easy way to eliminate prospective workers is to discriminate, and this is just what most unions have done.

> If you're white, you're right.
> If you're brown, hang around.
> If you're black, get back.

Until recently, you could have counted the number of black union electricians, plumbers, carpenters, bricklayers, and doctors on the fingers of one of Jimmy Hoffa's well-fed hands. Blacks have realized this and now form their own unions.

Any minority group that has overt physical characteristics (dark skin, big noses, slanted eyes) has also suffered at the hands of unions. They, too, try to form unions sometimes. Let's look at the Mexican-Americans' attempt at stopping exploitation by the California grape growers.

10

For Christ's Sake, Stop Eating Grapes!

For well over three years now Cesar Chavez' *huelga* has attempted to bring California fruit growers to their knees. The justice of his cause is obvious to anyone who has seen the deplorable shacks that the fruit pickers must call home. By any decent standard of living Mexican-Americans are existing with inhuman conditions. They should be asking for even more than their perfectly reasonable demands.

Let's assume the strike ends and Chavez gets all he demanded. Better houses will be built, grape pickers will have more money, and everybody will be happy.

But wait. If the same amount of grapes are sold at the same price that prevailed before the strike, won't the Capital-

43

ists be making lower profits? Surely, because their costs will have gone up. And we know Capitalists won't stand for that. They'll raise their prices to the stores, who will in turn pass on the increase to the consumer. Will people still buy the same amount of grapes? A lot may, but some may no longer be able to afford the increase in prices, while others may now think apricots a better deal for their money. Both groups will reduce their consumption of grapes.

When the stores start getting stuck with more and more rotting grapes, they'll order fewer. The Capitalist growers won't be able to sell all they're growing, so they'll grow smaller crops. Smaller crops require fewer harvesters. Are you beginning to suspect speed in your sunshine? Chavez will now be faced with the problem of rationing fewer jobs to the same number of *hermanos*. And Chavez' task won't get any easier as time goes on. The increased labor costs give growers additional incentive to mechanize.

In the long run, who benefits from the union? The union members who work, obviously. At whose expense? No one's? Hardly. When you take a bigger piece out of the pie, less remains. Perhaps Capitalists will just make lower profits. Perhaps, but not for long. If their profits are too low, they'll take their capital elsewhere. Never underestimate the mobility of the businessmen running our country.

The ones who pay the most are those Mexican-Americans who do not get work. They end up competing for jobs with nonunion workers and so are right back where they started—or worse!

But we all know that the wages being paid Mexican-Americans are not enough to provide even a bare minimum level of existence. How can we help them? The same way we should help anybody who's poor. Give them enough money to live decently. Give them educational certificates for their kids.

I want to help the grape pickers, so I eat grapes for breakfast, grapes for midmorning snack, grapes for lunch, grapes for midafternoon snack, grapes for dinner, and grapes

for that midnight raid on the ice box. In this way, besides helping the makers of Kaopectate, I help grape pickers. How?
Simply by raising the value of grapes and therefore increasing
the demand for grape pickers.

But I'm sure you'll still want to stop the exploitation of the
hard-working Mexican-Americans. Let's see though in what
sense they're being exploited. The dictionary defines exploitation as "selfish or unfair utilization." We know that everything
a Capitalist does is selfish, so *that* goes without saying. Is he
unfair, however? He doesn't force his workers to stay on. He
does pay them low wages, in fact, the lowest wages he can get
away with. Can you expect otherwise? Not in this country.
Every Capitalist is faced with the problem of how much to
charge for his products, how much to produce, and how much
to pay his workers. You can expect him to pay just enough to
attract only that number and quality of worker he requires,
and no more. But it just so happens that some workers will not
work for less than they think they're worth.

Don't fall into the same trap as did a well-known economist in his beginning textbook. Everybody doesn't have to
know the whole story in order to have people being paid what
they're worth. Just because studies in New Haven, Connecti-
cut, show that workers don't really know exactly what wages
are in nearby areas, this does not mean that people aren't getting a fair wage.

All it takes are *some* workers who find out that they're
being underpaid. Some of them might move to areas of higher
wages and leave exploiting Capitalists with too few workers.
To get these necessary extra workers, wages will have to be
raised.

Even if workers don't take the time to find out about
better-paying jobs greedy Capitalists will make them aware of
these opportunities. Why? Because you can trust a profiteer
to buy the cheapest labor possible. If workers happen to be
relatively cheaper in an adjoining city it pays some Capitalists
to offer them slightly higher wages as an inducement for some

of them to change location. Profit-hungry employers fighting for the cheapest labor around tend to drive low wages up to normal.

You're probably tempted to say that there's always an ample supply of workers, so I'm wrong. But if there is, why do we see so many help-wanted ads? Why do most companies have large recruiting staffs? Why do grape pickers get 75 cents an hour and not 15 cents or 1 cent?

The only meaningful way exploitation can be used to describe the plight of Mexican-Americans is in reference to the small amount of investing we've done in them. That is, they have not been educated enough to be more valuable to employers. But the way to solve this problem does not lie in unionization.

Automation, Technological Unemployment, and the Death of a Workingman

In a popular song of the day (which you probably won't be listening to when you read this in our society of planned obsolescence) the spirit of automation rears its ugly head:

> In the year 5555,
> Your arms hangin' limp at your side,
> Your legs got nothin' to do,
> A machine's doin' that for you.

Is automation really a recent phenomenon? I think not. It started when man first started breaking rocks with a club.

Is automation causing technological unemployment? To be sure. Every time a machine replaces a man the country suffers from technological unemployment. Is the problem getting any worse? If you read the popular press you'd think we were on the brink of disaster:

2000 LOSE JOBS BECAUSE OF ONE COMPUTER

YOU HAVE TO HAVE A HIGH SCHOOL EDUCATION TO COMPETE WITH MODERN MACHINES

WHOLE REGIONS DEPRESSED BECAUSE OF MACHINES

If, by some accident, you read the sophisticated Capitalist press, you'll get a different story:

AUTOMATION CREATES MORE JOBS THAN IT DESTROYS

THOUSANDS RELIEVED OF DRUDGERY OF CHECK SORTING

CONSUMER GOODS CHEAPER BECAUSE OF AUTOMATION

Who's right? Both sides contain grains of truth, but both ignore many of the realities. If technological unemployment is getting worse and worse, should we not see a larger and larger reserve army of jobless, as Marx predicted? If we look at the figures for the U.S. during the last 40 years, we find that unemployment has ranged from 1.4 percent to 7 percent, except for the Great Depression. (As an aside, the Depression never would have been Great had the government not freaked out completely: It raised taxes and caused a decrease in the number of dollars in use by 30 percent.)

As I write this, employment is the highest it's been in many years. (This may not be true by the time my words see ink: The Federal Reserve System has recently been feeding the economy at a slower rate than people have come to expect.)

Where, then, is all the technological unemployment we keep hearing so much about? It's all around us. People are always going to be put out of work by better technology. This doesn't mean that nobody will have anything to do in the year 5555. To say so is to deny two economic realities:

1. Given the opportunity, people prefer to be better off than worse off.
2. Human wants are unlimited.

Say a group of men are put out of work by an electronic mustache waxer. Most will probably prefer to look for another job. A few will find equally well-paying jobs, perhaps in a hair removal establishment. (Women, are you embarrassed by unwanted hair?) The rest may have a much harder time. They may end up receiving a lower salary and doing something completely different from their previous occupations. We can be sure they'll eventually find someone to sell their labor to (barring governmental interference) because human wants are unlimited. As fewer people are needed in manufacturing, more people will flow into the service sector of the economy.

Automation will cause people to work at different tasks; automation will not gradually eliminate *all* jobs.

As workers' real incomes grow, people may, as they have done in the past, decide to buy more leisure. They will work fewer hours and take longer vacations. Working less is not the same as not working at all and only presents a problem to a Capitalist: What are people going to want to spend their leisure time doing, and how can the Capitalist best make a killing by catering to those wants?

What can the government do to prevent technological unemployment? The only realistic answer is to provide more information on job opportunities and changing trends. In this manner the government can help workers choose jobs that will not immediately be automated out of existence. This information, when added to a minimum income system, will allow people to relocate to places where they can find the best jobs. More education would also assure workers of having greater job possibilities.

Is automation, this depersonalization of production, being forced on an unwilling public? I think not. Collectively, we do have the choice of buying personalized products created by hand craftsmen, for example. We all complain that "they don't

make 'em like they used to." Yet, do we collectively demand handcrafted products when given the chance to buy
mass-produced, usually cheaper ones? Obviously not. Just look
at the high death rate of artisan shops engaged in making
handtooled leather goods, handthrown pottery, and handtail-
ored clothes. We clearly must prefer the machine to the hand.

Are today's machinemade products crappier than those
you used to buy in the "good old days"? Before you say, "of
course," consider the following. You're given $1000 to spend
only on items from a Sears, Roebuck catalogue. You have the
choice of either using one from 1950 or from 1970. Would you
choose the one from the good old days?

Think about it.

The Hidden Persuaders and the Waste Makers or the Decline and Fall of the Affluent Society

Thanks to Vance Packard, Robert Theobold, and John Kenneth Galbraith we are all instilled with the conventional wisdom that Capitalists create wants so they can sell us products we don't need. After all, how could Americans have needed tailfins on their cars while so many were starving? How can Americans need color T.V. when so many are starving? How can Americans need any of the worthless things they now spend their money on while so many are starving?

Agreed, poverty should be eliminated, but its existence has nothing to do with created wants. When you look at what someone else buys and decide that he really didn't need it, you're imputing your value judgments to him. Somehow I feel

I have no right to pass judgment on other people's spending habits. Does anyone have the right to tell me I can't blow 40 bucks on Stones albums. Likewise, you may think speed's the greatest, while I swear by hash.

Let's look for a moment at the economics of that insidious monster, hidden persuasion. According to Packard and his crew of would-be economists, production somehow magically creates its own demand. This sleight-of-hand is accomplished through the medium of advertising. Once something is produced, the Capitalists will get you to buy it even though you don't want it, will never need it, and couldn't possibly use it. Assume for a moment that advertising can create wants out of thin air. A Capitalist has a choice among several different ways of screwing the public and will always try to find the most effective way. One of these choices involves using a little market research to find out what wants are not being satisfied by his competitors, then producing goods or services to capture the undeveloped areas. Perhaps he'd also advertise to inform the public that his product is now available.

Or he has the choice of producing something that isn't around and that people don't want but which he'll advertise so much that they'll end up thinking they need it. For this he'll need expensive sellout psychologists who use their knowledge of the secret workings of our id to trick us into irrational purchases.

Which path of action will the money-grabbing Capitalist choose? Of course the one that gets him the most profits. If he takes the least costly and least risky course of action, he'll cater to already existing wants. It's only logical.

Let's look at the possibility of actually creating wants. Do you really think a huge T.V. advertising campaign for merkins would send every female in the land screaming to her nearest department store demanding a half-dozen in assorted colors? And looking at the quarter billion dollars Ford Motor Company blew on the Edsel, and how much it was advertised, gives us dead proof that advertising doesn't always work.

If your and my behavior as consumers can be influenced

significantly by advertising, then "1984" is less than 14 years away. Something quite ominous lurks behind the money-making threats of the hidden persuaders. Those who cry "beware" imply that we are incapable of resisting persuasion, hidden or otherwise. In that case *all* our behavior can be altered by what we hear on the radio, see in the movies, and watch on T.V. If we accept this alarming possibility, then we must agree with California's bastion of wisdom, Max Rafferty, that the government has the obligation to make sure we don't read pornography and don't see sex and violence on T.V. or in the movies. The government needs to protect defenseless us.

If I had young kids I probably wouldn't want them to see close-up cunnilingus scenes on the tube. If they are being shown, I have the freedom either to send the children into the other room, turn off the T.V., or not have the screen in the house. So do you.

The same holds for almost all forms of advertising. I usually don't have to read, listen to, or look at anything I disagree with or disapprove of. Again, neither do you.

The minute you accept censorship of advertising you're paving the way for government Fascists imposing their uptight, puritannical, outdated values on the rest of society. Being unduly deprived of bare skin on the tube is one thing. Big Brother is another.

If we're going to be stuck continually with censorship, let's at least get some fair play into it. Let's limit tax-financed advertising that justifies Vietnam. And if truth in packaging is enforced for toothpaste and Wheaties, let's enforce truth in packaging for politicians. Why should those S.O.B.'s be allowed to promise us the world and then do what they damn well please once elected?

Hidden persuasion goes hand-in-hand with planned obsolescence. A bestseller in France asked: Is America Too Rich? We're supposedly near the point of total collapse because we have to make things fall apart in order to keep up our level of consumption.

This is equivalent to agreeing that human wants are

limited. They aren't. They're limitless. During the 1940s several New England economists fell into the trap of not believing this. They prophesied that the economy was speeding down a deadend road. All private investment possibilities would soon be exhausted. There would be no alternative left to the government but to take over a greater and greater part of the economy. Otherwise, we'd have permanently growing unemployment. These projections proved false, as do all that stand on the shoddy foundation of limited wants. If one thing about lowly man aspires to infinity it is his wants.

The idea of planned obsolescence really rests on the fallacy that people will buy the same total quantity of something no matter what its price. Consider a car. Let's say it can be made to last 3 months or 6 months. At the same selling price, the cost per month of the first one will be twice that of the second. You buy a car for the services it gives you. Most people, though certainly not all, will not buy a car when services are twice as expensive as what they would get elsewhere.

What does this mean? Simply that Capitalists must take into account the fact that products they make to last for a short while will not always sell well. The consumer will choose the products that last longer, if both have the same other qualities.

The producers know—and if they don't they learn the hard way—that if they charge too much for what they offer, other Capitalists will make a wad by undercutting them or offering a more attractive product at the same price.

This doesn't mean we don't have planned obsolescence. We do; but here's the rub. It's planned by the consumers and not the producers. Surprised? Just consider a moment. Clothing can be made to last many years, but people insist on new styles for summer, fall, winter, and spring. The same with cars. The fact that relatively unchanging VW's exist alongside Fords, Chevys, and Cadillacs just shows that some people don't value changing styles highly. In America this is a small minority, otherwise some U.S. car producers would provide us with the same style coffin year after year after year. People typically come up with the Packard-Theobald-Galbraith conventional wisdom because they want to show how shaky the Capitalist foundation is. I'd say the foundation was as shaky as the greed of the Capitalists who sit on it.

Those who claim that the artificial stimulation of planned obsolescence is necessary for the health of the economy also insist on the inevitability of its death when the war machine comes to a halt.

The War Machine that Keeps Our Country Running

If you look at the number of people employed by the military-industrial complex you probably realize that our economy would be up the creek without a paddle if all of a sudden there were no wars. Why, we'd have the same amount of unemployment as during the Depression.

We all know that wars are good for the economy. Look what World Wars I and II did for gross national product. Look how *GNP* keeps shooting up with Vietnam.

On closer inspection, though, aren't we leaving out a few facts? Weren't we in a recession just before World War I? Hadn't we just started pulling out of the worst depression in our history just before World War II?

What if instead of waging war on foreign Fascists our astute government had declared war on poverty at that time? If the same number of dollars had been shot into the veins of our faltering economy, would there have been less of a flash?

What about Vietnam? If we look at unemployment figures previous to our current large-scale attempt at genocide, we see that about 5 percent of the labor force was out of work, not the 14 percent we had before the outbreak of World War II. It turns out that the billions spent for Vietnam have caused Capitalists and government lackeys alike to fear "overheating" the economy. They're afraid the war will cause the economy to blow its lid.

What is the argument really about? It's about the inability of the private sector to sustain enough employment and to find enough profitable outlets for available capital. Therefore some kind of government cooperation with profiteering industrialists is necessary.

You should immediately be suspicious of this idea. It rests on the fallacy that human wants are limited and on the fallacy that Capitalists aren't smart enough to find more and more areas in which they can screw the public. To say that the private sector of the economy wouldn't know what to do with all the resources now being used in the war is to subscribe to these obvious misconceptions. If you wish, I'll personally oversee the spending of those billions. What I dream of doing is cutting taxes by $20 billion and letting people use them any way they wanted. I'd take the other $10 billion for the movement.

It's true that rapid demobilization would cause unemployment, but only for a short time. It took only a matter of months, not years, to find employment for virtually all the World War II veterans. We could set up another G.I. Bill, as we did after the Korean War. Our problem would then be overemployment of our colleges and universities, not underemployment of men.

To state that war profiteering exists is merely to harp on the well-known fact that whatever government does, it does poorly. To state that war is necessary for the economy, though, is to underestimate the flexibility of businessmen greatly. There would be no survival of the Capitalist species in our financial jungle if this were true.

Why Can't I Be a Rainmaker Too?

Having just discovered that powdered blue flats when shot from a cannon cause the rains to fall, I decided to go into the business of rainmaking. But I couldn't. Why? No license. You don't believe me? It's true; you gotta have a license to practice rainmaking. A cute little note in the *Journal* tells it like it is:

> GOTTA LICENSE? A growing number of jobs require you to have one.
>
> Occupational licensing by Federal, state, and local bodies increases sharply. The Labor Department estimates that 550 occupations are licensed by at least one governmental jurisdiction, double the number twenty-five

61

years ago. Recent additions to the list: pest-control experts, nuclear materials handlers, and fund-raisers.

Prostitutes, rainmakers, tattoo artists, bee-keepers and lightning-rod dealers are among today's licensed practitioners. Licensing often results from public outcries against unqualified or dishonest practitioners.

But that's great, you say. We shouldn't allow unqualified people to offer their unwanted services and wares to the unsuspecting public. Somebody should watch out for the consumer. Agreed. But who in fact does the watching?

Let's say that we don't want the poor sap coming in off the street to get hepatitis every time some tattoo artist sticks a needle in him. So we get the city fathers to pass a law limiting the practice of tattooing to licensed artists only. A nice little sign is painted on some door in city hall: TATTOO COMMISSION. What's missing? Obviously somebody to certify whether or not the tattoo artists pounding on the door for a license are qualified.

Who's going to do it? The mayor? His secretary? The city manager? The janitor? Hell, no. They don't know nothing about that type of skin game. The only people who do are those guys standing in line for a license. The city fathers must therefore get a few tattooers together to make up some standards to be used for licensing and to check everybody out on them. Fine, you say. Just pick the best tattooers in town for the job. Great, I say, but not for long.

At first everybody will probably be happy. Since those cats chosen for the commission feel pretty friendly toward others in the profession, only the obvious phonies will be denied a license. The buyers of colored skin are better off; they no longer fear hepatitis from tattoo quacks.

Let's look at the situation a few years later. Licensed tattooers are happy, but wouldn't mind making a little more money. All of a sudden the town starts getting more and more people. More sailors want tattoos. Tattooers are working hard; some are starting to work longer hours than ever before. They're not used to it. They decide that they should be compensated for their extra hard work, so the prices of their handiwork go up. Other artists will probably raise their prices, too. The higher price discourages some potential customers from getting needled, but certainly not all. With the same number of tattooers the increased demand from sailors allows prices to rise without any of the artists having less business than before.

Licensed tattooers end up making more money. They don't mind it and their wives and lovers are happy. Can this situation last? Well, aren't some other guys going to notice that tattoo artists are now driving new cars and eating in better restaurants? Some of those observant cats may think they wouldn't mind driving a new car, too. They'll want to join the skin game and may even start learning the trade from somebody who's already in it.

What's going to happen when they go to the TATTOO COMMISSION? A few will probably get certified with little trouble and a bit of bread under the table, particularly if they are cousins of the commissioners. But as soon as the tattoo artists on the commission realize that more and more tattooers will surely cut into the nice pie being eaten, licensing will come to a screeching halt.

Fine, you say, if unqualified skin men are prevented from ruining people's epidermi. But the trouble is that qualified skin men will also be prevented from working. The *Journal* article I quoted before mentions this:

> . . . Labor Department officials worry that the licensing power is sometimes used to keep qualified workers out of certain occupations. In one small community a licensing board dominated by plumbing contractors rejected 7 of 8 applicants for a license required to set up a plumbing business.

And have you ever wondered why there are so many gringos doing the plumbing, electrical, and masonry repairs in New York City's large Spanish-speaking ghettos? The reason is not hard to find: All licensing exams in that great city are given only in English. I'm sure you'll agree that the ability to speak English is important but not essential to threading a pipe, soldering a wire, or plastering a wall. Do you think that this capricious and discriminatory use of licensing powers is limited to a few exceptional cases? Let's look back to Joe Mc-Carthy's decade.

In various states during the early fifties the following occupations required the signing of a loyalty oath before certification was okayed:

1. boxing
2. wrestling
3. piano tuning
4. pharmacy
5. veterinary medicine

Was there a suspected Communist conspiracy to put all our pianos out of tune so that Americans could never win a Tschaikovsky festival?

Was there a suspected Pavlovian plot to inject our dogs and cats with Marxist-Leninism?

As contemporary evidence that licensing is still used to prevent people from exercising their guaranteed right to free speech and political opinion, we need only look at what has happened to Muhammad Ali, the world heavyweight boxing champion. He decided that he really didn't have anything against the V.C.'s. He said so publicly. He decided to refuse military induction into the killing machine because of his religious convictions and his position in the Black Muslim Mosque.

Do Muhammad Ali's views make him an unqualified world champion? Apparently so, for practically all the patriotic boxing commissions in the country refuse even to let him fight, let alone be champ.

Does your kid brother want to be an Artificial Insemination Donor (AID) when he grows up? Tell him he'd better hurry before someone licenses him out of a job.

Unsafe at Any Speed

I'm fed up with the cars in which tens of thousands of Americans are killed each year.

I'm fed up with the houses in which thousands are burned to death each year.

I'm not the only one. Many public-minded Congressmen have demanded, and sometimes gotten, more safety regulations put on the books. Cars can no longer come off the assembly line "unsafe at any speed." Building codes prevent rapacious contractors from putting up houses with chintzy wiring, leaky plumbing, and dangerous heating.

I say that not enough has been done. It seems that by the time the right building codes are added to the books somebody has invented something safer and better. To find out why this is happening, let's look into the political economics of governmental construction standards.

Just as consumers have complained to the government about unqualified and unethical practitioners, so they have complained about shoddy cars and houses. Since everyone agrees these products shouldn't be put on the market if people are going to die in them, our city, state, and Federal governments have decided to make up a set of standards to which all cars and houses must conform.

For certain aspects of production even the guy on the street can tell you what should be required. Cars must have seat belts and padded dashes. Houses must be built with good ventilation and well-constructed electrical wiring.

How much more can the layman say? Can he tell the building code commission what width of seat belt is safest? Can he explain which gauge of wire has the least chance of overheating and causing a fire? Can he say what thickness of plaster should be used for proper heat retention?

I think not.

Who, then, must ultimately go about adding all the minute details to our building codes? The experts. Who are the experts? Obviously the men who manufacture and repair houses and cars.

But there's nothing wrong with that. Just get together the most qualified and most public-minded contractors, plumbers, bricklayers, steering wheel makers, seat-belt weavers, and tire dealers. Have them all meet with some Congressmen to work out a set of specifications that will insure the buying public of the highest quality of product possible.

This is all fine and good. Standards are set up and all must abide by them. But wait. We don't live in a static world. New things are invented every day. What happens when Potter's Plaster, Inc., discovers a new material that's three times stronger, ten times more resistant to cracking, and four times cheaper than anything on the market? I'm sure you'll agree that many people building homes will want to use Potter's new plaster. They'll save money and have better walls to boot.

But they can't use it. Why? Because of the building codes. When the standards were set by the experts they had no idea that Potter was going to come along with something new and upset the apple cart.

But surely the code can be changed, you say. Yes. But not before many moons. You can be certain that the makers of regular plaster will have their lobbies paying off every legislator in town. You can be sure that the masons' union will have their lobbies supplying whores to any legislator in town; after all, Potter's plaster can be put on in one-half the time it takes to put on regular stuff. That means less work for union masons.

The end result is a set of regulations which benefit everyone but the consumer. Some consumers do, however, get what they want; and so we have, for example, beautiful mobile home camps springing up like gold in an Acapulco farmland. The more building codes there are, the more expensive regular homes seem to be. So people who want cheap homes turn to relatively unregulated glorified trailers. Dollar for dollar, those tin apartments are a better deal because most of the construction is done without regulation on an assembly line, using relatively lower-paid nonunion workers. Mobile home-makers, therefore, produce without much restriction what will sell the best; that is, what the public demands the most.

Building codes also have a habit, like state constitutions, of being added to but never being subtracted from. So we end up with costly additions to our cars that are unnecessary: If I'm wearing the over-the-shoulder seat belts required on my car, why must I pay for a padded dash and a collapsible steering wheel?

Why don't building codes work? The answer is easy. Special interest groups, like producers and repairmen, have concentrated, well-defined goals. They can attack with vigor any changes in legislation that will harm them. Consumers, on the other hand, have millions of goals as the buyers of products.

They are a diversified group of people who cannot collect forces easily to fight legislation that may affect the production of only a small aspect of what some of them are buying.

The moral of the story: Give special-interest groups a chance to screw you and they will, and probably where you'd least expect it.

Danger: This River a Fire Hazard

Could the pilgrims ever have imagined that the rivers they were pissing in would eventually become fire hazards? Their urine wasn't *that* potent. Today's industrial piss is. So much inflammable waste has been flushed into some rivers that they could literally go up in flames.

Pollution is all around—in the air, on land, at sea. True, it's taken man many years to reach the exalted state where he can make ski slopes out of garbage dumps. To make sure that we start things right in other worlds $12 million worth of junk was left on the moon after "mankind's greatest achievement." (Hell, I thought it was the invention of the Pill.)

Since the most obvious pollution comes from the belching

smokestacks of Bethlehem Steel, Kaiser Aluminum, and Dow
Chemical we usually blame the whole mess on Capitalists'
greed. If they didn't want to make so damn much money
they'd be more careful. Right?

Let's look at the situation a little more closely. The profiteering Capitalist isn't the only one making our air unbreathe-
able and our water undrinkable. Have you ever seen the way
houseboat dwellers dispose of their garbage? Do you know
how many car owners purposely disconnect their antismog
devices? Have you ever taken a stroll on the beach after a
Fourth of July weekend?

All these examples serve to demonstrate the underlying
economic reality: Whenever the cost of people's behavior to themselves is less than the cost to society, we're in
trouble. The roaches you left on the beach probably don't
cause you much concern, since you may never return. But the
straight who walks his pure-bred afghan there every day may
not feel the same way. You, and everyone else, who leaves crap
on the sand imposes a cost on other people who like to see
clean beaches.

When I fire up the engine of my Ford, I probably don't
smell much exhaust. But when all of us get together in downtown L.A.—well, you know what happens.

When you buy a groovy copper waterpipe the cost to you
is less than to society, because the copper mill probably stinks
up the air when it refines the metal for your pipe. As yet, concerned individuals haven't been able to band together in order
to force copper mills to pay for the suffering they cause (watery
eyes, emphysema). You therefore don't pay for that particular
aspect of production when you buy the pipe.

Most pollution problems do have technically feasible solutions. Since these solutions seem too far off for some people,
other more drastic ones are sought after. For example, California is attempting to ban internal combustion engine use by
the mid-seventies. And conservationists want all steel plants to
close down, or at least relocate to the Sahara.

I see an easier solution: Tax enough to insure equality of

private and social costs. If your local steel mill is causing too much lung cancer tax it and use the proceeds for air filtration. If beach fans insist on leaving beer cans around charge them an entrance fee in order to pay for cleaning the sand. Don't say it won't work. Germany started to tax manufacturers according to how much crap they dumped into the Rhine. The purity of the water has been increasing ever since.

It does little good to question a man on how much he values such things as pure rivers and clean beaches. If he thinks you might end up charging him something he'd naturally say he's not interested. Why? Because he hopes the rest of us will pay the full fee. This is called the "free rider" problem.

DeGaulle loudly proclaimed France's desire to make her own way in the world. NATO ended up one country smaller. Since DeGaulle knew that in time of war the NATO powers would come to France's aid, he shrewdly chose to become a free rider on NATO's defensive horse.

True, it may not always be feasible to impose taxes on the guilty ones, but other possibilities exist.

Some feel that cities are polluted by too many human bodies. If this is so we can at least offer legalized abortions and present deserving mothers with pills and gold coils.

A complete scientific solution to pollution may be just around the corner, but don't count on it. Unless polluters can be made to pay the full price of their actions, we will never see an end to the problem. Our stinking society can no longer let its conscience be its guide.

Medical Care: The High Cost of Maintenance and Repairs

It isn't enough that millions of Americans don't enjoy a bare minimum standard of living. The system has also made sure that they're not even given adequate medical care.

The inflation of doctors', dentists', hospitals', and pharmicists' prices in recent years is a fact of which we are all aware. Health, Education and Welfare officials have recently proposed a solution to the spiraling price rise: Broaden the coverage of medical insurance to all Americans. Public-minded M.D.'s have asked their fellow healers to show more moral responsibility toward the public. Still others have proposed socialized medicine. England did it; why can't we?

As if high prices weren't bad enough, sometimes you can't

even *find* a doctor. Why are there so few doctors and dentists? To understand why, we must first go back to the analysis I gave for unions and licensing.

It so happens that doctors in this country have the strongest union around. They call it the American Medical Association. (The dentists have their own organization.) You must realize that the doctors' union is no different than the garbage collectors' union; a union by any other name smells the same.

Doctors have an extremely effective way of limiting the supply of medical care: They certify medical schools. Why is this important? Because anywhere a person wants to practice medicine he has to have a license. How does he get one? By being a graduate of an approved medical school. Since the list of approved schools in each state is identical to the list approved by the A.M.A., you can see immediately that the doctors' union has complete control over the sources of new doctors.

Doctors have used this control wisely. The number of medical students admitted each year is many times fewer than the number of applicants. (Note that there would be even more applicants if people didn't think it was so hard to get into medical school.)

When the U.S. has at times received an influx of foreign doctors, such as after Hitler's rise to power, the A.M.A. made sure that these foreign competitors couldn't get licensed for practice.

And what union has consistently discriminated against blacks? The A.M.A.

Doctors will tell you the number of medical students must be limited and that many years of training must be required in order to maintain the high quality of medical care in the U.S.

Despite some facts to the contrary (like one of the highest infant mortality rates in the Western world), it is true that our doctors are among the best "qualified."

Is this what we really want? I think not. Does a rural housewife need someone who's gone through 4 years of college, 4 years of medical school, 1 year of internship, and 2 years of residency to give her a prescription for birth control pills? The point I'm making is that not all of us can afford, or need, or even want highly qualified medical practitioners.

In order that the wealthy can obtain, without much trouble, the best in medical care, the rest of us are denied the possibility of getting our machines serviced at a reasonable price. True, we can go to relatively lower-priced chiropracters, osteopaths, and faith healers; but most of us are suspicious. Any regular M.D. will gladly tell you that those guys are charlatans who shouldn't be allowed to exist. Would you expect him to say otherwise? Those "quacks" are taking away some of his business.

Limiting the supply is not the only way doctors screw us. I'm sure you're familiar with many medical practices that come under the heading "ethics." A wise man once said: "When someone mentions ethics, watch out. He's going to screw you within the next five minutes."

Most so-called ethical questions in medicine involve nothing more than a code of noncompetition. Doctors and dentists are not supposed to compete for customers, as do dope peddlers, ice cream manufacturers, and condom makers.

Why is it unethical for doctors and lawyers to advertise in the newspapers and the Yellow Pages? Because they'd be competing for patients.

Why is it unethical for doctors and dentists to make public their schedules of fees? Because they'd be competing for patients. Don't fall into the trap of thinking that the demand for medical service is not influenced by the prices charged to, or the income earned by, the public. Much of American spending immediately after World War II was funneled into postponed demands for medical and dental services, thus showing that not all medical care is essential and that much of it can be put off.

Now that you realize that the supply of doctors is limited by the monopoly practices of their union, you can understand the absurdity of most schemes to increase public medical care.

What will happen if medical insurance is extended to all? The same thing that happened when Medicare was initiated: The price of medical services skyrocketed. Why? Because with a limited supply of doctors (and hospitals, too) the sudden increase in demand could only mean one thing: an increase in price. The reason there's been relatively high inflation in medical prices can be traced to governmental attempts at giving more people more help without breaking up the controlling monopoly that limits the supply.

How can socialized medicine bring us more medical care if the A.M.A. is still allowed to control entrance into the healing profession?

The next time you see your friendly physician let him know the cat's out of the bag: His union leaders are screwing society, especially that part of it unable to overcome Capitalist exploitation.

Rich Nation, Poor Nation

Just as there are the haves and the have nots among mortals, so there are the haves and the have nots among nations.

Just as there have been governmental attempts at changing the situation among men, there have been similar attempts at changing the situation among nations.

Just as there's been total failure with one; there's been total failure with the other. The gap between the rich nations and the poor nations has been getting bigger, not smaller.

But how can this be? Our magnanimous government has given billions away in foreign aid. We've helped countries out right and left. (Just look at the Dominican Republic, Cuba, and Thailand.) Why, everytime there's been a famine threatening somewhere we've come across with millions of bushels of wheat.

The sad reality, though, is that we've done more harm than good, especially regarding our well-received gifts of food.

What can underdeveloped countries usually do more cheaply than developed ones? Grow food. Since countries, just like people, usually specialize in what they're comparatively better at doing, you'd expect to see poor countries putting much of their effort into food production. You'd also expect them to be supplying the richer, more industrialized nations with some of this food in exchange for manufactured goods.

International trade figures tell a different story. Today, North America and Western Europe export much more food than they import. But how can this be? Shouldn't we be trading industrial products for agricultural goods, since we have a comparative advantage in producing the former? The answer is we would be doing just that if it weren't for government intervention.

America likes to help her farmers. As I told you before, what originally started out as a program to aid poor farmers has ended up a mess. Because of the tempting incentive of artificially high agricultural prices fixed by our government, U.S. farmers have grown more and more food. Not all of this food could be sold to Americans. In an attempt to keep our surpluses down the government has showed all sorts of ingenuity. We sell our food abroad at lower prices than at home. We prevent imports from competing with home-grown crops. And we even give food away.

You may think that giving "surplus" food to needy nations helps them out. It does; but only for a short time. If you were a farmer in India who sold wheat, how much could you sell when America had just shipped over 8 million bushels for free? Probably not as much as before, if you insisted on charging even close to your usual price.

To sell all of your crops you'd probably have to lower your prices drastically. Just as American farmers responded to high prices by producing more, Indian farmers respond to low prices by producing less. By giving away food America has succeeded in destroying a system of signals (called relative prices) which was telling Indian farmers when to grow more food.

Americans have another way of "helping" poor nations out. It's called foreign investment by some (United Fruit Company), and exploitation by the rest of us. You wouldn't believe the wages paid to Latins for picking your Chiquita bananas. You wouldn't believe the houses they live in or the rotten food they end up eating. I sometimes wonder how United Fruit can get anybody to work under such conditions. But ask Mr. Chiquita and he'll feed you some phoney line about conditions being even worse before his arrival and wages being even lower elsewhere. I'll believe that one when I see it.

All the government crap about "helping poor countries to help themselves" has been just that—crap. Since we've saddled ourselves with unrealistic domestic programs and unworkable international agreements we've succeeded in keeping poor nations where we want them—in poverty.

The Greatest Show on Earth

I'm sure you'll all agree that we have the richest government in the world. Its budget exceeds $190 billion. Even if the generals get $80 billion of that a lot is left over to help us out. We can put on the greatest show on earth.

Why is our government so rich? Obviously because it taxes a rich nation. Fine, you say, tax the rich to give to the poor. But if you don't know in your heart you know in your wallet that's not happening. In 1966 over 60 percent of the individual income taxes collected were from families making less than $15,000. It doesn't look to me like the rich are paying for much of it at all.

Another point should be made clear. Even if our government is the richest in the world, it does not have an endless supply of resources. What does this mean? Simply that the programs you think Congress should adopt will take governmental dollars away from someone else's projects. The guy telling you we can't do without better, safer highways is merely trying to get more tax dollars for his cause taken out of the total pie. The Senator rapping about necessary school construction is also fighting for part of that pie. When anybody tells you we absolutely need something, watch out. He's merely using a hard-sell argument to cop a bigger piece of the tax revenues.

But people have to eat, someone says, so the government must help the farmers.

Manufacturers have to have steel, so the government must help steel makers.

Kids have to be educated, so the government must help out schools.

Children have to get vitamins, so the government must provide free milk.

If you ask enough people what we need and who the government should help, you will soon end up with a list covering every industry and occupation and person that exists in this country. Since the number of tax dollars in any one year is not only limited but is coming out of our pockets, you know that our government cannot subsidize everything.

Who gets subsidized? The cats with the most political power. Let's look at the classic example.

The farm bloc in Congress has passed some of the most messed-up legislation ever, as I've mentioned before. The ultimate in helping out the poor farmers happened when a North Dakotan was subsidized to reclaim a few thousand acres of unproductive land. He did his work well and finished in a year. Then he decided to take advantage of another program; he put his beautiful, fertile, reclaimed land into the government's soil bank! Tax dollars are now being paid to him for *not* growing anything on land that tax dollars paid to have recovered.

And one California grower selling over $12 million worth of fruit a year receives in excess of $280 thousand, in addition to his usual profits, for not growing certain crops.

You'd think that the farm bloc would be weaker today than ever before, since we have just 5 percent of our population growing things for a livelihood.

That's what you'd think, but you'd be wrong. A perfectly reasonable bill to limit subsidy payments to $20,000 per farmer didn't even get off the Senate floor.

And after an investigation showed that most government-provided free milk was going to private schools for rich kids, nothing happened. They're still getting free milk. "After all," said one astute Congressman, "rich kids suffer from malnutrition, too."

What lesson can you learn from the farm program? As always, that given a chance your government will put on the greatest show on earth, a show of rich men screwing poor men.

A Plea for Anarchy

In your reading of the previous pages did you gradually get that vague feeling that something was rotten in the hallowed halls of our nation's capital? Did you start to realize that your favorite Senator might be taking you for a ride? Well, you were right. The reason things are not any worse in this messed up land of ours is in spite of, not because of, the country's leaders.

We have a representative government. It represents the rich oil man, the rich cattle raiser, the rich wheat grower, the rich steel producer, the rich doctor, the rich dentist, and the rich lawyer. If you ever got anything good out of your government you can be sure that some rich sonofabitch got even more by letting you get yours.

It's amazing how we all turn to Big Brother whenever there's a problem. We consider a Congress to be good if it passed lots of legislation. Have you ever stopped to analyze that legislation? If you did, you'd realize that ours is a government of special-interest groups, all trying to take the most away from everyone else. How can things be otherwise? Our pie can't get any bigger today, although it does grow slowly over time. What someone takes; someone else doesn't get. A cursory glance at the results of the past 194 years of legislation will show you who's usually gotten what and at whose expense —the rich at the expense of the poor.

True, there are many public-spirited leaders around. They really do want to help the poor, the black, the farmers, the kids, and the grape pickers. But the forces of economic reality are too strong.

What starts out as a great program to help poor farmers ends up being a fiasco that makes rich men richer and saddles consumers with higher taxes and larger food bills.

What starts out as a great program to protect the poor worker from the powers of the large corporation ends up as carte blanche for putting down the black man.

What starts out as a great program to encourage oil exploration ends up as a tax haven for wealthy Texans.

What starts out as a great program to educate all our kids ends up as a reverse Robin Hood.

What starts out as a great War on Poverty ends up as an army of highly-paid self-righteous bureaucrats.

What starts out as a great governmental program ends up a mess. You thought the moon shots were worth it? Well remember what the first guy there said: "One small step for man, one giant leap for government."

Since the government's messed everything up, should we get rid of it? The revolution followed by anarchy? Before you leap with joy, consider what would happen. Now we have a so-called democracy with a constitution and majority rule.

The only reason the minority can hang around is because its rights are protected by the constitution. These rights are, to be sure, not always fully defended by the government.

For anarchy to work, however, all members of society must be fairly homogeneous. There would be open season on wops, wetbacks, kikes, niggers, hippies, polacks, redheads, and cripples if the constitution didn't exist. I happen to want to keep my hair long and curly. You may not want ever to wear shoes. The only way to prevent the majority from forcing us to change is to have some guarantee of our rights enforced. Anarchy is not the answer. We should therefore keep government, but reduce its power over our economic, moral, and social lives.

What should we do, then, to solve our problems? Demand only a few simple realistic programs from the powers that be— enforcement of contracts, protection of constitutional rights, a minimum income, and the distribution of educational taxes by way of certificates. Anything more complex will only give every rotten profiteer in the country a chance to fatten his purse at our expense.

My plea is clear
. . . less government today
even less tomorrow.